KSENIJAI -
LAI DZĪVO FRANCIJA !

VECTĒVS
UN
VILMA

1997.G. 18.MARTĀ

A PORTRAIT OF
FRANCE

Lee Server

Euredition

This book was designed and produced by
Todtri Productions Limited
P.O. Box 20058, New York, NY 10023-1482
according to a proposal from Euredition bv, Den Haag

Editions of this book will appear simultaneously in France,
Germany, Great Britain, Italy, and the Netherlands
under the auspices of Euredition bv, Den Haag,
Netherlands

This edition published by Euredition bv,
Luiksestraat 23, 2587 AL The Hague, Netherlands

ISBN 90 75082 05 3

Author: Lee Server

Producer: Robert M. Tod
Book Designer: Mark Weinberg
Editors: Mary Forsell, Joanna Wissinger, Don Kennison
Production Co-ordinator: Heather Weigel
Typesetting: Mark Weinberg Design, NYC
DTP Associate: Adam Yellin
Printed and Bound in Singapore by Tien Wah Press

PHOTO CREDITS

Photographer/Page Number

Peter Bastaja 16, 35 (bottom), 39, 48 (top), 80, 86, 87
Kul Bhatia/Picture Perfect USA 90
Randa Bishop 23, 34, 35 (top), 114, 116, 120-121
John Blake/Picture Perfect USA 46
Charles Bowman/Picture Perfect USA 10, 11, 13, 18, 19, 21, 22, 26, 28 (top & bottom), 29 (top), 30, 37, 38 (bottom),
   43 (top), 51, 53, 54, 55, 56-57, 58 (top), 59 (top), 65, 66, 67, 68, 71, 75 (bottom), 83 (top), 84, 85, 106 (bottom),
   122-123, 123 (right), 124, 134
Jean S. Buldain/Picture Perfect USA 52 (top), 76 (bottom)
Bullaty Lomeo 5, 38 (top), 42, 44 (bottom), 50 (top), 52 (bottom), 61, 64 (bottom), 74, 76 (top), 99, 101, 110-111, 128-129
Sonja Bullaty 14, 15, 70 (bottom), 102-103, 106 (top), 108, 109, 112 (top & bottom), 115
Mike Buselle/Picture Perfect USA 81
Haraldo de Faria Castro/FPG International 77, 125
Cornish/Picture Perfect USA 143
Robert Cundy/FPG International 27
James Doro 7, 118, 119
Ric Ergenbright 8-9, 59 (bottom), 60, 63, 72-73, 78, 83 (bottom), 97, 138 (top), 142
Robert Fried 6, 17, 24-25, 29 (bottom), 36 (top), 43 (bottom), 44 (top), 48 (bottom), 50 (bottom), 58 (bottom),
   82 (top & bottom), 92, 93 (top & bottom), 117, 126 (top & bottom), 127, 129 (right), 130-131, 132 (top & bottom),
   133, 135, 136-137, 138 (bottom), 140, 141
P. Frilet/Stock Image 94 (top)
Alan Hipwell/FPG International 49
Bill Holden/Picture Perfect USA 139
Doranne Jacobson 64 (top)
Julius Kharpoff/FPG International 95
Michael Krusowitz/FPG International 45
Ken Laffal 36 (bottom), 100, 104-105
Larime Photographic/Dembinsky Photo Associates 40-41
Graham Lawrence/Picture Perfect USA 69, 70 (top), 75 (top), 79, 91, 96, 98
Angelo Lomeo 62, 107
Guy Marche/FPG International 31, 94 (bottom)
John Miller 88-89
Richard T. Nowitz 32-33,
V. Pcholkin/Stock Image 20, 47
Charles Waite/Picture Perfect USA 113

TABLE OF CONTENTS

Built in the sixteenth century, the royal palace of Fontainebleau is a relatively subdued landmark compared to the wildly opulent Versailles Palace.

Introduction

*F*rom the rough seas and grey skies of the northern coast to the warm sunshine and lux- urious beaches of the Côte d'Azur, from the sophisticated shops and hectic pace of Paris to the timeless simplicity of an Alpine mountain village, France is a land of variety and contrasts. A modern economic giant and atomic-age military power, its fascinating histo- ry is reflected in the country's daily life. It is the land where chic, legendary fashion houses offer couture designs for handsome prices, and yet students and secretaries on a budget maintain a seemingly effortless elegance of style. In France, the restaurants include many of the most acclaimed and expensive to be found anywhere. Yet at any ordi- nary village bakery or grocery, a few francs buy delicious breads, pastries, and produce.

While most first-time visitors to France confine themselves to Paris and its environs— perhaps making a stop at one of the fabled resorts of the Riviera—each region of the country is rich in geographical, historical, and cultural attractions. On this tour in words and pictures, travelling from Paris to Provence, from the Loire Valley to the peak of Mont Blanc, the rich variety of this alluring nation unfolds.

Ancient Times

There is very little recorded history about ancient France except for references about the region garnered from other cultures. From about 500 BC on, the Greeks and later the Phoencians, Romans and other cultures traded with the people of these French lands;

needless to say, many conflicts ensued. These foreign kingdoms coveted Mediterranean trading posts such as Marseilles and Avignon, and eventually others farther to the north. But most of the area we now know as France was then controlled by the Celts, who had swept over most of northern Europe. Eventually, however, the Celts (known to the Romans as the Gauls) suffered from a lack of military organisation and were conquered by the much more efficient Roman army of Julius Caesar in 52 BC. All of Gaul, as France was then known, came under Roman rule with the Pax Romana, or Roman Peace. For the next several centuries, there was little anarchy or conflict in Gaul, as the land and its inhabitants became cultured, civilised, and orderly—in other words, Romanised.

Eventually, Gaul's centuries as a valued member of the Roman Empire ended, as did the empire itself. The Roman army was overrun by numerous German tribes who reaped much devastation on the land, including the destruction of the city of Metz. In 496, the Franks of Germany, led by Clovis, their king, emerged as the survivors of all these conflicts and were left to rebuild the war-torn land of Gaul, which then became known as the Frankish Kingdom.

The Middle Ages

Clovis began a line of French kings, known as the Merovingian Dynasty, who ruled France with mixed results for several centuries. This dynasty's rule resulted in an eventual breakup of the country into several different factions controlled by different fragments of the ruling family. This came to an end in 732, when the country became united under Charles Martel, who repulsed a great threat to the land made by warring forces of Islam, defeating them in a

In the French Alps, snow is seen all year round. At several areas in the mountains summer skiing facilities are available.

6

battle between Tours and Poitiers. Power was then concentrated in his hands. Thereafter, his son Pepin the Short assumed the throne. His reign was followed by that of his son Charles, later known as Charlemagne.

Not since the days of Caesar did one man dominate the European continent as did Charlemagne. His military successes reached in all directions, controlling the Mediterranean and all areas to the North Sea. Eventually, on Christmas Day in the year 800, he was crowned the first Holy Roman Emperor. His acceptance into this court of many scholars and artists shifted the cultural centre of Europe to the Frankish Kingdom. But this era did not last long, as the period following Charlemagne's death saw many more conflicts, much of it caused by the invading armies of the Norse Vikings. For several centuries to come, France's prosperity was lost in the Dark Ages.

At the annual Nice Carnival—the Riviera's version of the New Orleans Mardi Gras and Rio's Carnivale— a young woman rides a flower-bedecked float. The event takes place twelve days before Shrove Tuesday and draws celebrants from several continents.

By the tenth century, France was dominated by the manorial system, with manor lords so powerful that the reigning kings had no control over them. But gradually, both the monarchy and the church increased in strength. From the tenth century into the fourteenth century, the line of French kings known as the Capetians greatly expanded their kingdom's power, utilising shrewd judgements as well as some military might. By the end of the Capetian dynasty in 1328, their royal domain had been expanded by more than forty times. The influence of the Christian church also expanded during the same period. There were major reforms and reorganisations within the ecclesiastical structure, which enabled the church to invigourate education and scholarship and to bring to an end the centuries of barbarism of the Dark Ages. Many great monasteries and cathedrals were built, gaining strong influence over all matters.

Foremost was the monastery of Cluny, in Burgundy, which for more than five centuries was the largest and most significant structure in all of Christendom. The following centuries saw the construction of the Cathedral of Notre Dame in Paris, as well as those of Chartres, Reims, and Amiens, among many others.

Renaissance and Reformation

During the fourteenth century, the Capetian family's rule over France died out after more than three hundred years, resulting in a bitter battle for control of the kingdom. Capetian heirs in both England and France claimed title to the crown, resulting in the bloody Hundred Years' War, which actually lasted 116 years—though not continuously—from 1337 to 1453. Following several English victories under Henry V, France's existence seemed doomed. This led to the Treaty of Troyes in 1420, which surrendered much of the nation to its conquerors. Though the country was in ruins, Charles VII, a recent successor to the French throne, refused to accept English domination, and with great help from Joan of Arc's battlefield leadership at Orléans and Patay, France's fortunes in the long conflict changed. Though Joan was eventually captured and burned at the stake by the English, the French military successes continued. In 1453, the Hundred Years' War ended, as the English were finally driven from the country.

The long, brutal war resulted in the near destruction of the feudal class in France, but this

allowed Charles VII and his successor, Louis XI, to establish a strong royal authority in a newly organised and now unified country. When Louis XI's successor, Charles VIII, married the heiress to the duchy of Burgundy in 1491, all the lands we now know as France had become a part of the kingdom.

In 1559, King Henry II was accidentally killed in a tournament. His unexpected death weakened the French monarchy and resulted in decades of civil unrest. The situation was greatly exacerbated by the revolt against the Catholic Church. Spread throughout Europe by Martin Luther and John Calvin, the revolt reached France in 1559. The violence and despotism in France during the years of these religious wars between the Protestant forces—known as the Huguenots—and Catholic groups were said to be more brutal than anything seen even in the days of the Hundred Years' War. Perhaps the bloodiest moment came in 1572 with the mass murder of Huguenots, now known as the Saint Bartholomew's Day Massacre. The Huguenots regrouped, however, and eventually got the better of the conflict, though they were unable to capture Paris. The war concluded when a Protestant with claims to the crown, Henry IV, assumed the throne and converted to Catholicism to appease his enemies in Paris. In 1598, he issued the Edict of Nantes, which established religious tolerance. The rest of his days on the throne were spent restoring the monarchy to its previous glory.

Henry IV was the first in a long line of Bourbon kings, who would rule France for two centuries through times of glory as well as excess and bankruptcy. During the seventeenth century, two ministers of the government obtained enormous control over the affairs of state. Henry IV had been assassinated in 1610, and his successor, Louis XIII, was too young to assume the throne. Eventually, Cardinal Richelieu, whose original name was Armand Jean du Plessis, duc de Richelieu, won the confidence of the youthful Louis XIII and became essentially the ruler of the country. Richelieu's leadership was often vicious and usually cold-blooded, but successful on all fronts. Not only did he strengthen the monarchy

from within by curtailing the power of the nobility and the Huguenots, but he also led France to significant military victories, primarily against Austria and its ruling Hapsburg family. He greatly expanded the French navy as well, and by the time of his death in 1642, all of France's borders had been firmly secured.

Richelieu's successor was Jules Mazarin. He was originally from Abruzzi, educated in Rome by the Jesuits, and sent to Paris as a papal nuncio. During his years as France's prime minister, he was disliked for his supposed trickery and craft, as well as the huge wealth he accumulated. But he was a very able minister who was responsible for much consolidation of French power. When he died in 1661, the young king, Louis XIV, confiscated his huge wealth and assumed power himself, something not seen during the nearly forty years of dominance by Richelieu and Mazarin.

As Louis XIV reached his maturity, France entered yet a greater golden age. The country was the preeminent power in Europe, and Louis XIV celebrated this lavishly, building for himself a palace of immense grandeur at Versailles. He also patronised the arts on a grand scale, backing such notables as Jean Baptiste Racine, Molière, La Rochefoucauld, Charles Le Brun, and Jean Baptiste Lully.

In the waning years of Louis XIV's long reign, however, military reversals abroad resulted in the country's fall from its position of absolute dominance. Numerous foreign conflicts drained the nation's treasury, with the bulk of the needed funds coming from the poor, greatly reducing their standard of living and greatly increasing the levels of starvation and disease. Louis had also revoked the Edict of Nantes, which sent hundreds of thousands of Huguenots from the country, further weakening France's productivity.

A street scene from the Left Bank of Paris reveals that, unlike many other modern capitals, Paris has not become a concrete jungle. Trees and flowers flourish everywhere, and there are small parks in all neighbourhoods.

After Louis's death, the monarchy entered a period of decline, as did the country. Throughout the eighteenth century, France fought in many more costly wars, though they took place outside the country's borders. Nonetheless, court life under the new king, Louis XV, continued on in similarly lavish ways, as even more royal palaces were constructed for the king in Paris. But during this period known variously as the Age of Enlightenment and the Age of Reason, the intellectuals of the day in France—including Jean-Jacques Rousseau, Voltaire, Denis Diderot, and Montesquieu—began publishing works that called into question the social fabric of France. While the great thinkers of the previous century—such as Blaise Pascal, René Descartes, and Michel Eyquem de Montaigne—had never questioned the established and traditional authority, the eighteenth-century intellectuals promoted rational enquiry of man's nature and spoke of the good of unhindered thought, often quelled by the repression of the monarchy.

Bronze statues in Lourdes depict a scene from the life of Christ. The city contains one of the most important shrines in the Christian world.

Revolution

During the reign of Louis XVI in the latter half of the eighteenth century, the country's involvement in foreign conflicts—particularly its intervention into the American Revolution, along with a poorly devised system of taxation and a great deal of waste—had left France nearly bankrupt. Despite concessions to the clergy and nobles that reformed political and social conditions, Louis XVI was not able to quell the revolutionary spirit. The situation was additionally aggravated by a bad harvest in 1788, which made grain scarce and bread very expensive. On July 14, 1789, an angry mob stormed the Bastille prison. Soon after, the French assembly abolished the longstanding feudal structure. Still, the problems of the country continued. Eventually, the king's position grew even weaker. He was imprisoned in August 1792 and executed on January 21, 1793.

Meanwhile, throughout the country and particularly in Paris, anarchy—or more correctly, angry mobs—ruled. In what is now known as the Reign of Terror, one group massacred all those they believed to be against the revolution. This violence soon spread throughout the nation. The three main leaders of the movement—Georges-Jacques Danton, Jean-Paul Marat, and Maximilien de Robespierre—were all swept up in the violence themselves, and all were killed during the revolution.

Napoleon

By 1795, the country came under the rule of the Directory, but its period of rule was subject to much corruption and inefficiency, as well as high inflation and bankruptcy. Eventually, in 1799, Napoleon Bonaparte, who had led the French army to great triumphs in Italy and Egypt, was the beneficiary of a coup d'etat that saw him take over control of the government, now known as the Consulate, with Napoleon as the First Consul. Energetically, he soon brought inflation under control, restored the Roman Church to France by the Concordat of 1801 with Pope Pius VII, and established the first modern code of law, known as the Code Napoleon. He also continued to lead France to military successes, defeating Austria, Prussia, and Russia. Pius VII crowned him as Emperor in Notre Dame Cathedral in 1804.

By 1807, Napoleon was the clear master of Europe, but in 1812, when he began an assault against Russia, the lone unconquered nation on the continent, his empire began to crumble. Even though the French forces were more than 500,000 strong, their lack of supplies and adaptability to the winter climate forced them to retreat from Moscow. Eventually Napoleon's army was routed, and in 1814 he suffered another defeat at Leipzig, as his enemies became better organised and were able to take advantage of his weakened forces. In April 1814, Napoleon abdicated the throne, and was exiled to the island of Elba off the coast of Italy. But he returned to France the next year and was once again able to seize power. However, this reign only lasted about one hundred days before his forces were defeated in Belgium during the Waterloo Campaign. A coalition force led by the Duke of Wellington sent Napoleon into permanent exile on the British island of Saint Helena, where he died in 1821. His body was returned to France in 1840.

After the final exit of Napoleon, the French monarchy was restored, though most of the nineteenth century consisted of unending revolution and overthrow. There was the July Revolution of 1830 and the February Revolution of 1848, as well as the establishment of the Third Republic in 1870 after the country's disastrous results in the Franco-Prussian war. This republic lasted until the occupation of the country by Hitler in 1940. But amid the almost constant political upheaval, there were also years of culture and glitter. In an era known as La Belle Époque, Louis Napoleon, Napoleon's nephew, ruled France as

Nîmes is a city filled with remnants of ancient Roman occupation. Most impressive of these is the stone Amphitheatre. Better preserved than the Coliseum in Rome, the Amphitheatre once hosted bloody contests between gladiators and wild animals.

Emperor Napoleon III from 1852 to 1870, along with his wife, Empress Eugénie. Paris again became a centre of art and glamour. During these and somewhat earlier decades, Victor Hugo, Honoré de Balzac, and Charles Pierre Baudelaire wrote and Jacques Offenbach composed. In 1875, the Paris Opera House was constructed (it was the world's largest theatre); in 1889, the Eiffel Tower was built (it was the world's tallest structure). There were also great accomplishments in science, most notably through the works of Louis Pasteur and Marie Curie.

During most of the seventy years of the Third Republic, Paris was clearly the cultural centre of the world, being the home of such artists as Toulouse-Lautrec and Paul Cézanne and writers such as Émile Zola and Marcel Proust. Artists and intellectuals from all over the world came to Paris to work, including Marc Chagall, Pablo Picasso, Igor Stravinsky, and Sergei Diaghilev. Paris was also the centre for many American writers during the 1920s, including Gertrude Stein, Ernest Hemingway, and F. Scott Fitzgerald.

Modern Times

In the twentieth century, France's long history of military conflicts continued with two world wars fought against invading forces from Germany. With the technology of modern weaponry, however, World War I and World War II were much more devastating than any previous encounters. For many centuries, France had been the most populous country in Europe, but by the start of World War I, this distinction had been taken over by Germany, which, in a war of overwhelming attrition, was a large advantage. But with help from English and eventually American troops, France was able to survive the conflict, fought mostly on its own land. Germany, which had anticipated a quick win in the conflict as had been the case in the Franco-Prussian war of 1870, surrendered in 1918, four years after the beginning of the war in 1914. But France had about two million dead as a consequence of the war, and nearly a million more permanently disabled. Much of the agriculture and industry of the country was also devastated.

For the next twenty years, while Paris again became a great centre of culture and education, the country could not resolve its many political factions into unity. Nor had it developed enough military strength to combat another invasion by Germany. The forces of Hitler invaded in 1940, and within two months, France surrendered. During the next four years, French resources were used strictly to benefit the German military. The horrid years finally ended with the invasion of the Allied forces in June of 1944. France was liberated later in the year.

France was again a devastated land as the war ended. Charles de Gaulle, a French general who had refused to acquiesce to German control and had led the resistance during the war, triumphantly returned to Paris as head of a provisional government. France again showed its amazing recuperative powers—as it had for centuries, rebuilding its industrial base, with such companies as Renault and Air France prospering, though under control of the government. Political squabbles, however, continued unabated after World War II. Over a period covering nearly twenty-five years, de Gaulle was in and out of power several times. This period also saw major difficulties for France's widespread colonies in Africa and Asia. By 1965, de Gaulle had relinquished French control of virtually all of its international holdings, though only after experiencing difficult and damaging rebellions in Vietnam and Algeria. After those problems found resolutions, de Gaulle was finally voted out of office in 1969, following a tumultuous period of labour and student unrest. In subsequent years, France, under governments of various political persuasions, settled down as a prominent member of the European Community in the Nuclear Age.

A pretty view of the much photographed and painted Sacre-Coeur, the basilica with the Oriental-style domes. From this vantage point, the view of Montmartre below is spectacular.

Paris

*F*or travellers of today, as for those of the distant past, there are few destinations in the world so eagerly anticipated as the French capital. Paris is a dazzling fusion of the aesthetic, the sensual, and the historic. No other locale has ever had quite so many attractive superlatives and claims attached to it: the most beautiful and romantic city, home to the the greatest restaurants, grandest hotels, most esteemed museums, and even the most exciting nightclubs and greatest variety of cinemas in the world.

Paris, like all modern world capitals, is not the place it was a hundred, fifty, or even twenty years ago. The great, relatively earth-bound architecture of past epochs, the palaces and government buildings, the luxurious apartment houses and hotels—all have been overshadowed or replaced here and there by towering and anonymous skyscrapers. The unique blues and greys of the skies above Paris, much commented on by poets, songwriters, and more discerning tourists, have been altered by the fumes of industrial pollution. Neighbourhoods that once seemed like an inextricable part of the Parisian character, like the teeming nocturnal markets of Les Halles, the so-called belly of Paris, have been relocated to the suburbs, and are now just legends of the past.

And yet for all these and other changes, Paris remains essentially, ineffably the same experience for visitors of today as for those of decades and centuries gone by. It is the city of light, city of lovers, of cafes and elaborate meals, spacious boulevards and narrow, serpentine side streets, expensive couturiers and boutiques, sidewalk artists, and quay-side vendors selling cheap old postcards and used books. Through the centre of all this winds the River Seine, living symbol of Paris's remarkable continuity.

The Arc de Triomphe, or the Arch of Triumph, is 50 metres (163 feet) high and nearly as wide. Built by Napoleon (but completed during the reign of Louis Philippe in 1836), the arch is the site of the Tomb of the Unknown Soldier, dedicated to all who have died in battle.

A view of the interior of Notre Dame, designed in the Gothic style. It was here that Napoleon crowned himself Emperor and his wife, Joséphine, Empress.

First Impressions

Like all great cities, Paris is a set of contradictions. There are areas of great wealth and areas of poverty, places devoted to spiritual matters and others to concerns of the flesh. Divided into *arrondissements* or *quartiers*, Paris is composed of numerous distinctive neighbourhoods, all with their own separate—and occasionally notorious—characteristics. The visitor from abroad can sample a bit of each or be drawn to a single, compatible section and never leave it—the glamourous shops along the Champs-Elysées, watched over by the Arch of Triumph, or Arc de Triomphe; the busy metropolitan thoroughfares around the Place de l'Opéra, the grand boulevards of Madeleine, Capucines, Italiens, and Haussmann; the youthful and bohemian Latin Quarter, with its narrow, twisting back streets and throngs of students and artists (both real and delusional); or perhaps some tiny, unheralded corner of Paris the visitor takes pleasure in discovering for him- or herself.

For foreigners, a visit to Paris will probably mean arriving by air and landing at one of the city's major airports, Orly or Charles de Gaulle. Train rides from either airport bring the visitor the 14 kilometres (9 miles)—the distance from Orly—or 22 kilometres (14 miles)—the distance from Charles de Gaulle—through low-lying industrial and suburban areas to one of the city's major train stations. Although Parisians have a reputation for being among the most impatient of big-city citizens (in their defence, the residents claim, they are as rude to each other as to any hapless tourist), there are welcome conveniences in place for the visitor from abroad, including a government-run, hotel-finding service and a very user-friendly mass-transit system.

Paris is a city of nearly two thousand hotels, providing more variety of accommodations than any large city in the world. Government licensed and ranked from deluxe to a single star, the range of accommodations goes from the Ritz, the Crillon, the George V (hosts to kings, presidents, and movie

The winding course of the River Seine divides Paris into northern and southern parts. Indicating the importance of the river to the city's existence, the two halves are described in relation to the Seine as the Right Bank and Left Bank, to the north and south, respectively.

Works of art are a part of the fabric of Parisian life, whether they reside in the city's hundreds of museums or are sold on the streets— some by vendors, many by the artists themselves.

The avant-garde edifice known as the Centre Georges Pompidou has been a source of controversy since it opened in 1977. Built, according to some, to resemble the innards of an unfinished factory building, full of exposed tubing and skeletal pipes, the Pompidou is a museum for art works of the twentieth century.

stars) to aged, cramped little spaces on tiny side streets. As the city's luxury hotels are renowned, so, in a sense, are the best of her one- and two-starred offerings. Every seasoned traveller on a budget has their favourite secret find among the cheap hotels of Paris, some tiny but charming family-run place with a great view of Notre Dame, perhaps. There are bad hotels in Paris, of course; impersonal, antiseptic deluxe hotel chains, and one-star hotels one wouldn't wish on a prisoner of war, but on average Paris probably gives better value for money, at the high end or low, than any comparable city. Proof of this is in the number of visitors to Paris who return to the same hotel for decades.

Hotel reservations in hand, the visitor goes in search of a taxi. The drivers are not quite the stern taskmasters they are often made out to be, although their reputation was not helped any by the recent attempt to install electroshock systems in the cabs' back seats, the better to deal with 'unruly' passengers. If you're worried, it is nearly as easy and considerably cheaper to step down to a station of the Métropolitain, one of the greatest of all modern subway transit systems—cleaner and safer by far than New York's subway, more efficient than even London's Underground. At some stations, the above-ground entranceways retain their original Art Nouveau arches, railings, and ornately scripted signs.

Some stations play video programs for passengers awaiting trains, and at the station for the Louvre, the greatest and most legendary of the city's numerous museums, statuary and other works of art are displayed behind the platforms. The Métro's simple system of interconnecting lines needs only a minute or two to master.

Paris's most famous boulevard, the avenue Champs-Elysées, is densely lined with shops, restaurants, and cinemas.

The Grand Palais, built for the World Exhibition of 1900, was intended only for temporary use. However, this structure, with its steel and glass interior, has survived to serve as a major exhibition hall.

Tourists and locals enjoy an outdoor cafe along the busy Champs-Elysées. Along with the traditional French cafes and restaurants, the boulevard now offers assorted American fast-food chains.

The Eiffel Tower

Settled into a room and ready to explore the city, the visitor to Paris needs perspective, something provided by the upper reaches of the Eiffel Tower, Paris's most famous landmark and often used as a symbol of the city itself. As permanent an addition to Paris as it seems today, the tower was once considered merely temporary. Designed by Alexandre Gustave Eiffel and erected in 1889 for the Universal Exhibition, the structure was meant to be dismantled soon after. Some felt it was pointless; others complained of its colour and that it blocked the view. Yet the majority of Parisians warmed to its 298 metres (985 feet) of elegant, symmetrical metal lacework. The tower was for some time the tallest on earth. While its dismantlement was still discussed as recently as the early years of the twentieth century, such talk died away shortly thereafter, and there has been no further controversy regarding its permanence.

There are three levels to the tower. Most pay a nominal fee and go up by elevator, but for a 'hands on' encounter with the magnificently intricate construction, take the staircase. From the top one looks out on all of Paris. The view on a clear day is approximately 64 kilometres (40 miles) in any direction. The French came late and reluctantly to the age of the skyscraper, so there are relatively few modern highrises to block an encompassing view. Most of the city's buildings remain at pre-elevator heights, and depending on where you are glancing, the Eiffel's aerial panorama today is not so very different from what it would have been one hundred years ago. Below lies what appears as a scale model of the city come to life.

Explorations

Grand and varied as it is, Paris is also a relatively compact city compared to other major capitals of the world, only 99 square kilometres (38 square miles) in all, an excellent size for walking tours. As seasoned travellers know, only by foot can one really discover a city's true character, the serendipitous attractions never quite captured by a guide book—perhaps the aromas from a corner bakery passed en route, a charming bistro that is still undiscovered by tourists, or a tiny shop that catches the eye with such irresistible items as one-of-a-kind engravings, made-to-order lingerie, or French movie memorabilia. Expect your shoes to wear out, though, long before such a walking tour does, for there is much to see—a lifetime's worth, in fact.

Paris is roughly divided in half by the meandering Seine. While the division gives the city geographic northern and southern halves, these are referred to by their relation to the river as the Right Bank (to the north) and the Left Bank (to the south). What nature has bisected, the French further divide into twenty sections of the city, called arrondissements. There are things to be seen in each of these, but the key Parisian sights and landmarks lie within the boundaries of the First through Eighth Arrondissements, encompassing parts of both the Left and Right Bank, with the Fourth right in the middle of the river, comprising two small islands.

After the Eiffel Tower, Paris's most famous landmark is undoubtedly the massive Arc de Triomphe, the largest structure of its kind in the world. Begun by Napoleon in 1806, it is a tribute to French military victories and losses. Pageants and military parades have marched through the Arc countless times since its completion, including twice by the conquering armies of the Germans. Below the stone buttresses a flame burns at the Tomb of the Unknown Soldier, a rueful reminder of the many lives that war claims.

the Métropolitain, or more familiarly the Métro, is Paris's great underground transit system. Many of the entranceways maintain their original Art Nouveau signs.

After feasting their eyes on both the gargoyle-covered exterior and massive interior of Notre Dame, visitors can take in more spectacular sights at the top.

While the evening's event may be sold out, a daytime trip to the Paris Opera House is well worth your while—simply for the tour of the spectacular building itself, the largest of its kind in the world. The interior features a sweeping staircase, sculptures, paintings, glittering chandeliers, gleaming bannisters, and other glorious details.

The Place de la Concorde—partially taken over by a swirling traffic circle— is the former site of the revolutionists' guillotine. Here, King Louis XVI and Marie Antoinette, among others, were separated from their noble heads.

The Colonne de Juillet, with its statue of the winged god of Liberty, honours the victims of the 1830s July Revolution. It was built at the site of the notorious Bastille Prison, stormed by a mob on the first day of the French Revolution, July 14, 1789.

This distinguished-looking edifice is the Hôtel de Ville (City Hall) of Paris. The faux-Renaissance-style building was erected in the 1880s after the previous one had burned down.

Passenger boats offer tours up and down the Seine. Since so many important buildings and landmarks were built along this river, these cruises offer a unique view of Parisian history.

A dozen avenues radiate from the Arc, the most famous of them being the broad and busy Champs-Elysées. Some say the presence of countless cinema posters, fast-food hamburger chains, and the hordes of camera-toting tourists has ruined what was once a quietly elegant promenade, but for the majority, the bustle of commercial activity along this sumptuous street simply represents big city excitement.

At the other side of the Arc de Triomphe is the massive oval of swirling traffic known as the Place de la Concorde. It is the site of one of the bloodier chapters in Parisian history. During the French Revolution, it was at this place that the revolutionists' guillotine was kept busy and where Louis XVI and Marie Antoinette, among others, were executed.

France is justly renowned for its magnificent churches and cathedrals, and Paris is home to some of the best of these. Most famous is Notre Dame. Words—certainly no less than a dictionary volume's worth of them—can hardly do justice to the perfection of this Gothic architectural masterpiece, over a century in the making. The stunning exterior, with its looming towers, portal carvings, and its grotesque gargoyles is matched by the immensity and resplendence of the interior.

Among the city's other beautiful and historically significant places of worship are Sainte Chapelle, dating back to the thirteenth century, and once the official church of the French royal family. The stained glass windows here are perhaps the most beautiful in the world. The noble La Madeleine, not far from the Place de la Concorde, is a church with a chequered past, first a place of worship, then intended as Napoleon's secular Temple of Glory, then returned to use as a church.

A dazzling Gothic-designed church in the manner of Notre Dame, Saint-Severin is recommended for its collection of fiendish gargoyles, monstrous creatures and killer birds, and other fascinating faces of evil.

A view of the impressive façade of the Assemblée Nationale, the National Assembly or Parliament building for the French government. The tricolour has been the nation's flag since the Revolution of the late eighteenth century.

One of the oldest churches in Paris is that of Saint-Germain-des-Prés, with elements in its present construction dating back to the sixth century. Perhaps the most recognisable church after Notre Dame is the serene-looking Sacré-Coeur, located in the atmospheric Montmartre area. The church's Byzantine-style domes, towering over the fascinating street scenes of the district, have been featured in countless paintings and postcard images.

One more bit of sacred ground is a popular tourist attraction, not for any church built on it, but for what lies beneath it. The cemetery of Père-Lachaise holds the remains of a vast, multinational array of legendary names, from the star-crossed lovers of the twelfth-century, Heloise and Abelard, to the sixties' rock superstar Jim Morrison. Other permanent residents include Oscar Wilde, Honoré de Balzac, Georges Bizet, Sarah Bernhardt, and Edith Piaf. Despite the starry competition, the late lead singer of the Doors has been the most visited grave at the cemetery for many years.

Other popular attractions include the Conciergerie, a building with a varied history but most notorious as the dreaded prison run by the Revolutionaries, a halfway house of grim, painfully uncomfortable-looking cells for those who were on their way to the guillotine. Another building with Revolutionary associations is the Pantheon, first a church, then a shrine to the heroes of the Revolution, a church again, and finally a nonreligious shrine to the great names in French history. Emile Zola, François Marie Arouet Voltaire, and Victor Hugo are among those whose tombs are honored by inclusion in the Pantheon.

There is no better proof of Paris's romantic allure for many visitors than in the continued popularity of tours in the sewers of Paris. No doubt

The Moulin Rouge in Montmartre is the nightclub-theatre made famous by Toulouse-Lautrec in the late nineteenth century. Each night the painter sat at his table and sketched the musicians, rowdy dancers, and cancan girls.

Approached from any direction, the magnificent exterior of the Louvre prepares one to encounter art from a broad range of styles and periods including some of the masterworks of Western civilization.

Place des Vosges was one of the city's first formally planned squares, and the commercial buildings around it contained one of the first shopping arcades. Among its many uses through the years, the Place des Vosges was once the city's most popular site for duels of honour.

Residing on a hill above the picturesque streets of Montmartre, Sacre-Coeur is one of Paris's most recognisable structures. Distinguished by its Byzantine domes, the church has been depicted again and again in paintings of Parisian street scenes.

With its Corinthian Greek façade, the Church of the Madeleine was once intended to be a nonreligious shrine to honour Napoleon's army. Its grand interior is lit by three large glass domes.

A façade detail from Notre Dame Cathedral. The exterior contains a series of sculpted portals. Higher on the cathedral are its fiendish-looking carved gargoyles.

The awe-inspiring Gothic cathedral of Notre Dame took over a century to complete. It is known to literature as the haunt of Victor Hugo's tragic creation, the hunch-backed bell-ringer.

Sidewalk cafes are a fixture throughout Paris, and a stop at one for a coffee or aperitif is usually a part of every Parisian's daily ritual. Seen here, the famous Deux Magots on the Boulevard Saint Germain, a favourite haunt of writer Ernest Hemingway.

Food is, of course, taken very seriously throughout France. Speciality shops, such as the one seen here, offer exquisite delicacies, laid out in tasteful settings worthy of a parfumerie display.

with images of *Phantom of the Opera* and *Les Misérables* in their heads, hundreds line up twice weekly for this fascinating visit to what is quite literally the city's underworld.

Paris has resisted becoming a concrete jungle in the manner of other large cities, and greenery is visible everywhere you go. The city's actual parks range from the carefully and beautifully tended Jardin des Tuileries to the wild and sprawling Bois de Boulogne. With the city's long months of mild weather, Parisians spend much of their leisure time out of doors, particularly at the sidewalk cafes that are an integral part of Parisian social life. Some of these cafes—De La Paix, Deux Magots, and the like—are rich in associations with great painters, performers, and writers of the past. As a result, they have become tourist attractions to rival the major monuments. The top cafes are not inexpensive, but for the price of a coffee or soft drink you can sit for as long as you wish, enjoying the passing parade or perhaps invoking the days when Ernest Hemingway or Pablo Picasso might be seated at the next table.

The Les Halles section
of Paris was once the
tumultuous all-night
marketplace for wholesale
meats, fish, and produce.
This lively, legendary
subculture was eventually
moved to a less colourful
suburb near the Orly Airport.

A stone sculpture at
Place Rene Cassin in
the Jardin des Halles
is one of the many that
can be found in public
spaces throughout Paris.

The Luxembourg Gardens,
originally created for the
occupants of the adjoining
palace, is now one of the
most beloved and popular
public sites in all Paris.

Here visitors to the Louvre ponder the works to be seen in the museum's Grande Galerie. The Louvre has holdings of a quarter million works of art, though, of course, not all of these are masterpieces.

Although the Louvre has seen maniacs attack and damage its most famous display, Leonardo's Mona Lisa, no exhibit at the museum has caused wider controversy than the new addition seen here. It is I.M. Pei's notorious pyramidal entrance structure in the courtyard.

Museums

Paris's pleasant street life makes it difficult to go inside, but the city's array of museums is justly famous. No trip would be complete without a visit to one or two, or perhaps a dozen—a fraction of the more than one hundred major museums and exhibitions open to the public. First and foremost is, of course, the Louvre, with its collection of a quarter million works housed inside a vast palace beside the Seine. The museum's holdings—which include *The Winged Victory*, the *Venus de Milo* and, of course, Leonardo da Vinci's haunting portrait of the *Mona Lisa*—cover six separate departments, from furniture to Egyptian antiquities.

Other museums offer works from a narrower range of history, and sometimes from a single artist, such as the Rodin Museum, the Delacroix, and the Musée Picasso. The Musée d'Orsay, a renovated train station, is the home to some of the best work of the Impressionists, displaying masterpieces by such artists as Pierre Auguste Renoir, Edouard Manet, Vincent van Gogh, Edgar Degas, and Paul Gauguin. Twentieth-century art works are represented in the Musée National d'Art Moderne, and in the ever-controversial, factorylike structure of the Centre Georges Pompidou.

Paris's range of rewarding museums extends beyond those showcasing only the traditional fine arts. The Musée de l'Armée chronicles French military history, while the Musée Carnavalet is devoted to the history of Paris itself, displaying personal effects of kings and other notables, as well as vivid recreations of Parisian life in the past, including the long-destroyed Bastille, the infamous pre-Revolutionary prison. This century's own art form, the cinema, has its origins captivatingly laid out at the Cinémathèque museum near the Palais de Chaillot, with rare examples of the first motion picture cameras and films on display along with photos, documents, and assorted ephemera from the primitive stages to the modern era of the motion picture.

The Louvre was originally a fortress, but it was rebuilt as a royal residence in the sixteenth century. Enlarged over time, it began its role as an art museum with the coming of the French Revolution.

Napoleon's tomb is a sarcophagus of red porphyry. Also entombed at the Dôme des Invalides are several members of Napoleon's family and Marshal Foch, leader of the Allied armies during the World War I.

*The sprawling Hôtel Des Invalides houses the
Musée de l'Armée (Military Museum) and
the tombs of Napoleon and other French leaders.*

The most important modern artist in the field of sculpture was Auguste Rodin, and many of his best works are displayed at the Rodin Museum, an eighteenth-century mansion where the artist lived and worked.

A group of students passes through the grand hall of the Musée d'Orsay. One of Paris's many spectacular and unusual settings for the display of art, the building was in fact formerly a railroad station.

Sculptor Auguste Rodin's most famous work, The Thinker (Le Penseur), is the leading attraction at the Rodin Museum in Paris. The statue, seen here, is located in the courtyard where visitors enter the museum.

LE PENSEVR
DE. RODIN OFFERT
PAR SOVSCRIPTION
PVBLIQVE AV PEVPLE

The gardens at Versailles are carefully tended to maintain the perfection that French monarchs had come to expect when they resided at the legendary palace.

Amid the unreal opulence of the Hall of Mirrors at Versailles, the Treaty of Versailles was signed.

Countryside Excursions

In the countryside outside Paris are some of France's most attractive and significant sites. At Versailles and Fontainebleau, respectively 24 kilometres (15 miles) and 64 kilometres (40 miles) from Paris, one enters the dreamlike world of the French monarchs. The unreal opulence of the Versailles Palace is a wonder to behold, from the dazzling Hall of Mirrors to the extravagant landscaping of the gardens. The smaller Fontainebleau Palace was built in the midst of a vast, wild forest, the private hunting grounds of monarchs from the sixteenth century to the time of Napoleon.

Two delightful excursions from the capital are to the Monet house at Giverny, and the charming château and race track at Chantilly. In the house and garden where Monet lived, one can take in the living inspiration for the master Impressionist painter. Surrounded by shimmering garden lakes, Chantilly's blue-roofed château is a masterpiece of the architect's art. The race course at Chantilly is simply the most elegant place of its kind, even when crowded with hordes of screaming bettors.

A bit farther from the capital—though still little more than an hour's travel time by train—is the medieval city of Chartres and its fabled Gothic cathedral. Dating back to the twelfth and thirteenth centuries, the cathedral took thirty years to build and is the greatest remaining testament to the devotion and skill of the craftsmen of the Middle Ages. Remarkably, many of the thriving homes and shops of Chartres are equally ancient.

Not far from Paris is the fabled Palace of Versailles, a very real wonderland built for the French monarchs. To tour all of its many rooms and gardens would take an entire day.

Beautiful Giverny, an hour's drive from Paris, was the home of the Impressionist painter Monet. His charming house and flower-filled garden are now a museum open to the public.

Another view of Monet's pink house and the colourful flowers that inspired him. Monet often painted on a barge in the middle of the garden pond.

The Fontainebleau Palace is set in a forested area 64 kilometres
(40 miles) south of Paris. The woods, some 20,000 hectares (50,000 acres)
of them, were once the private hunting preserve of the French monarchs.

Following page:
Sunset over the
River Loire, near
the city of Blois,
creates a tranquil
scene. Rich in
associations with
the French monar-
chy, Blois for a
time was a place
of banishment for
bothersome rela-
tives of the kings.

The greatest heroine
in French history, the
teenage Joan of Arc,
led a victorious army
in the liberation of
besieged Orléans. She
was later captured and
tried by the English, who
burned her at the stake.

The Loire Valley

*B*efore 1600, around the time when Paris became the hub of power in France, the Loire
Valley had been the country's centre of civility and royalty.

The region surrounding
the Loire Valley is one
of the most charming
and picturesque in all
of France. Medieval
villages, such as
St-Charité-sur-Loire,
are a vision of serenity.

Orleans and Chinon

The Loire Valley was the home of Joan of Arc, who was born in Domrémy, but became the
heroine of Orléans, which still honours her accomplishments abundantly. The city named both
a chapel and street in her honour and placed a statue of the heroine in the main square (Place
du Martroi). Her residence during the siege of Orléans in 1429 has been restored and is now
a tourist attraction, full of relics and information about her life. The city's souvenir stands are
also overflowing with Joan of Arc merchandise.

Well to the west of Orléans—along the River Vienne in the southern part of the region—is

South of Paris 96 kilo-
metres (60 miles) is
the medieval city of
Chartres. Here one
finds the stunning
Cathedral of Chartres,
dating back to the
early thirteenth century.
The cathedral's stained
glass windows, with
their 'Chartres blue'
colourations, are
believed by some to
be the most beautiful
in the world.

The golden altar
and statue inside
Chartres Cathedral
were erected
after the cathedral
was completed.

Chinon, another town in the Loire Valley that was greatly involved with the history of Joan of Arc. There is not much left to see in Chinon now except for the ruins of its towering fortress castle. But during the Hundred Years' War, the fortress was the location where Joan met Charles VII, and convinced him of the prospects of her mission. Chinon also contains a bell tower, the Tour De Horloge, constructed in 1399, which also offers a Joan of Arc museum.

The strategic location of the Loire Valley has had a great deal to do with its involvement in many conflicts in ancient times and the Middle Ages. Orléans, lying to the north of the river in the extreme northeast corner of the valley, was the successful target of invading armies of both Julius Caesar and Attilla the Hun. In the Middle Ages, the Loire River itself was of vital importance to the French for transportation, and its waters were also very useful as an aid in preventing foreign invasions. The large fortress at Chinon is just one of many constructed atop the multitude of high hills in the region.

The Loire River wends its way along the city of Orléans, once the home of Joan of Arc. Many of the city's ancient buildings were destroyed in bombing raids during World War II.

Atmospherically rich, the medieval town of Chinon contains the fortress-like château that was the residence of Charles VII. It was to Chinon and this diffident Dauphin that Joan of Arc came to seek an army.

Loire Châteaux

Because of the gentle nature of the region's hills and waterways, many generations of French rulers found the Loire Valley the perfect location to build or acquire their royal palaces. So plentiful and spectacular are the castles that the region became known as the Loire Châteaux. Centuries after their construction and use, many of the lavish castles are much too expensive to be individually maintained. Instead, they are now under the care of state and local governments who have preserved these landmarks for their historical significance. And, especially in the summertime, the Loire castles are now host to numerous public events, including concerts and sound and light displays known as *son-et-lumière*, which attract huge crowds to the region.

Perhaps the most noteworthy of all castles in the Loire Châteaux is that of Chambord, about 48 kilometres (30 miles) to the west of Orléans. It was constructed in the midst of a royal game forest under the rule of Francis I, although he spent little time there. It was also utilised occasionally by Louis XIV, who viewed performances of plays there, including Molière's *Le Bourgeois Gentilhomme*. The castle's construction started in 1519, and took more than twelve years—some say twenty-one—to be completed. Many critics have considered the castle at Chambord to be excessively extravagant, with more than three hundred chimneys, more than four hundred rooms, and with a façade more than 121 metres (400 feet) long. Its popularity with tourists, however, is unquestionable. Following the French Revolution, the Chambord château entered a lengthy period of neglect, until it became one of the castles operated by the state. Visitors now move about the structure freely as kings did centuries before.

A Loire Valley castle equal in popularity to Chambord is in Chenonceaux, to the south of the Loire along the Cher River. Also constructed in the sixteenth century, the castle at Chenonceaux is noted for its charm and tranquillity, set amidst a river and a garden. It now houses works by such artists as Paul Rubens and Antonio Allegri da Correggio. The castle is also closely linked in history with the castle of Chaumont. King Henry II had given the Chenonceaux Castle to his mistress, Diane de Poitiers, but after the king's death in 1559, his widow, Catherine de Medici, insisted on the palace for herself. So she bought the Chaumont château and exchanged it with Diane for Chenonceaux.

Another of the most notable castles in the Loire Valley is in Blois, right along the Loire, about 16 kilometres (10 miles) to the west of Chambord. Blois itself, like much of the valley, is still an extreme contrast to the bustling cities of France and elsewhere, with its hilly terrain and colourfully crafted houses. The castle itself contains features constructed over several centuries. It was most utilised by Louis XII, Francis I, and Francis II. The most notable feature of the Blois château is its spiral staircase, built, like so many of the valley's structures, during the reign of Francis I.

Another of the many beautiful châteaux of the Loire is the exquisitely graceful Renaissance creation found at Azay-le-Rideau, on the idyllic banks of the Indre River. Built by one of the ministers of Francis I, the king became so enamoured of the beautiful building that he soon took possession of it.

The fourteenth-century Castle Sully in Sully-sur-Loire has numbered Joan of Arc and the exiled Voltaire (for whom the resident duke built a theatre) among its guests.

Chambord, by far the largest of the Loire Valley châteaux, was completed in 1519, after more than twelve years of construction. It contains over four hundred rooms, and the surrounding grounds and forest measure 5,200 hectares (13,000 acres), encircled by 32 kilometres (20 miles) of wall.

The château of Chaumont in the Loire Valley, built by Charles d'Amboise, was once the residence of both Catherine de Medici, widow of King Henry II, and Diane de Poitiers, his mistress. The two women lived there at separate times, however. The château, like so many in the valley, is now government owned and open to the public.

To the west of Blois along the Loire is Amboise. Its famous castle was a royal palace during the fifteenth and sixteenth-centuries. It was Charles VIII who oversaw the beautification of the castle, though ironically, he was killed when he bumped his head on a stone archway overhanging a door. The site of this accident is still on display for those touring the structure. The castle itself is not what it was then, however, or later, when Francis I made it his royal court. Much of the castle was levelled, and less than half of the original building remains.

The castles of Chambord, Chenonceaux, Blois, and Amboise are all situated in the eastern part of the valley. However, there are also a number of famous sights in the western half of the region. The Loire Valley is about 224 kilometres (140 miles) long, beginning with Orléans to the west and concluding near the town of Angers in the east. Angers, just north of the Loire on the River Maine, features a huge medieval fortress constructed in the thirteenth century. In later years, the harsh nature of the structure was softened considerably by the additions of flowers and wildlife on the grounds, as well as a chapel constructed in the sixteenth century. Other sights in Angers include the Cathédrale Saint-Maurice, built in the twelfth and thirteenth centuries, mostly in the Gothic style though with some Romanesque touches as well. The museums of Angers include works by Raphael and the noted local sculptor Pierre-Jean David.

Another famous châteaux along the western edge of the Loire Valley is in Plessis-Bourré, which is about 16 kilometres (10 miles) to the north of Angers. Built in the fifteenth century, the château of Plessis-Bourré has the exterior of a typically stark fortress, with an unusually long moat of about 45 metres (50 yards). But inside of its walls the mood is much different, primarily because of the extravagant depictions painted upon its wooden ceilings. Yet another distinctive structure in the western half of the Loire Châteaux is in Saumur, about 96 kilometres (60 miles) to the southeast of Plessis-Bourré, on the southern side of the Loire. The town is now quite noteworthy for its huge harvest of mushrooms, which is reported to be in the millions of pounds. Its fourteenth-century white château, however, with its fanciful gates and plentiful flowers, stands tall over the town and the river.

Another famous castle in the region is in Ussé. Its château is famous for its various colourful and carefully built towers and turrets. Farther east in Azay-le-Rideau, there is another white château most note-

Each area of the renowned gardens of the Villandry château is uniquely beautiful. The gardens are on several levels of the château grounds, each with its own design or floral speciality.

Villandry, 18 kilometres (11 miles) from the city of Tours, is home to this château, built in 1532 by Jean Lebreton, architect for King Francois I. The U-shaped château is most famous for its spectacular gardens.

worthy for its magical park area. Still another famous castle farther to the east is in Saché, which was built from the sixteenth to the eighteenth centuries. Its atmosphere is more that of a very comfortable country house than of a palace. It is most famous as Balzac's home during the 1830s. The writer's work at the château is celebrated in a large Balzac museum on the grounds, which includes original manuscripts, artifacts, and photographs.

Because of the grandiose nature of the Loire châteaux, they became very important warehouses during the German occupation of World War II. The castle of Chenonceaux became one of the largest repositories of art treasures which were stored away from Nazi grasp. Another such sanctuary for art work was to the south of the region in the dungeons of Loches, which, centuries before, had been used as torture chambers by King Louis XI.

Tours and Environs

There are many other sights to see in the Loire Valley besides its castles. About 16 kilometres (10 miles) west of Saumur, for example, is the town of Fontevraud and its famous medieval abbey, which was constructed in 1099. For more than six centuries, the abbey of Fontevraud played an important part in the history of France, and such historical figures as Henry II of England and his son Richard the Lionhearted were entombed in the abbey. After the revolution, Napoleon turned the abbey into a prison, which it remained until almost 20 years after World War II, when the government decided to restore it to its historical state, a project still in progress.

About the midway mark of the valley is the largest town, Tours, which, unlike almost anywhere else in the area, is a modern metropolis of more than 150,000 people. Nonetheless, it contains a number of historical sites, most notably its Cathédrale de Saint-Gatien, built from the thirteenth to the fifteenth centuries. Its most famous features are its façade of two towers—which have been recently restored—and its stained glass. There are some notable museums in Tours as well, including the Musée des Beaux-Arts which features works by Rembrandt, Rubens, and Degas, among others. Tours also offers a wine museum, a guild museum, and a wax museum, the Historial de la Touraine, which has more than 150 wax models of historical figures of the region, including Joan of Arc.

The château of Chenonceaux in the Loire Valley was the pawn in a notorious royal love triangle. Henry II made a gift of Chenonceaux for his mistress, Diane de Poitiers. When Henry died, his wife, Catherine de Medici, became the regent of France and promptly took possession of Diane de Poitier's residence, banishing the former mistress to the smaller château at Chaumont.

The fifteenth-century château at Amboise is
grandly situated nearby the Loire River. Here a
future king of France, Charles VIII, son of
Louis XI and Charlotte of Savoy, was born in 1470.

Great natural beauty, unspoiled villages, and such fabulous châteaux as Château Montigny-sur-Loir are the major attractions in the Loire Valley. So much of the area has remained unchanged through the centuries that visiting it is like a journey back in time.

Normandy
and Brittany

*T*he two northern regions of France bordering on the English Channel and the Bay of Biscay, Normandy and Brittany both have traditions that vary from the rest of the country and are equally fascinating in their histories.

A Turbulent History

Normandy was conquered in the tenth century by the Norsemen, or Normans, as the region's name indicates, with the Duke Rollo being given control of the land in 911. In 1066, Duke William of Normandy conquered England and became that country's King William I. As the English kingdom then grew stronger and more independent, subsequent kings fought with France for control of Normandy for several centuries. The land was permanently restored to France in 1450.

Much of Normandy was devastated during World War II, as it was the site of a great deal of the fighting in the liberation of France in 1944, including the D-Day invasion on its shores. One of the hardest hit cities was Caen, on the narrow Orne River in the Department of Calvados, less than 16 kilometres (10 miles) from the English Channel coastline to the north. Caen was the favored residence of William the Conqueror and his wife, Matilda, as well as the city where William erected the Abbaye aux Hommes and the Abbaye aux Dames as penance to receive papal consent for his marriage. Both structures still stand, and the Abbaye aux Dames contains Matilda's tomb.

The Abbaye aux Hommes did contain William's tomb, but it was destroyed in later times by the Huguenots. A thigh bone was salvaged, though, and re-entombed, only to be destroyed later by eighteenth-century revolutionists. Other landmarks in Caen survived until the World War II bombing, which destroyed both William's castle and the city's university, founded in 1432.

The ancient capital city of Normandy was Rouen, which remains the capital of the Seine-Maritime Department. It is the city where Rollo established his capital in 911 and the site at which Joan of Arc was burned at the stake in 1431, when the city was under English occupation. The exact spot of the immolation is permanently marked in the pavement in what is now a central market area of the city.

In subsequent years, Rouen became a great centre of both scholarship and religion. Rouen has also been one of the major port cities in all of France, at times handling more shipping merchandise than any other French port. It has also been long famous for its cuisine, with many famous restaurants, some of which were, like

The greatest attraction in Normandy, indeed one of France's most spectacular sights, is Mont-Saint-Michel. This granite wonder, capped by a magnificent Gothic church, is connected to the mainland by a narrow causeway.

A sixteenth-century brick church along the windswept coastline of Brittany is testimony to the enduring power of religion in the region.

Brittany's rugged peninsula offers great opportunities for those visitors who enjoy hiking tours. Many of the rural stretches of the region are virtually untouched by time.

At Carnac in Brittany, visitors can view the field of giant megaliths. These huge stone placements are considered among the greatest known remnants of ritual behaviour by prehistoric man, although the exact purpose of the display remains a mystery.

much of the city, destroyed during World War II, but soon after restored.

Rouen architecture is dominated by ecclesiastical structures, though they are almost completely Gothic in style, built from the thirteenth to the fifteenth centuries, rather than in the eleventh-century Norman style. These include the famous churches of Saint Maclou and Saint Ouen. The most prominent structure in Rouen is the Cathedral of Notre Dame, which is famous for its contrasting towers. It also contains the tomb of Rollo.

Another major port city in Normandy is Le Havre, in the southwest corner of Seine-Maritime, at the mouth of the Seine. Le Havre was founded in 1517 and is a very busy, working-class city, with a population of about 200,000, about twice that of Caen or Rouen. Nearby are the popular resort towns of Trouville and Deauville, in the northeast corner of Calvados. These cities were also hard hit by World War II artillery, but both were well restored afterwards. Thousands crowd the beaches of these towns, particularly in August, when world-class thoroughbreds compete at the Deauville racetrack.

In addition to its ancient structures, resorts, and ports, Normandy is also a centre of agriculture, with much dairy farming and cattle raising. There are also vast apple orchards that not only form a large industry but add to the scenic beauty of the

A centuries-old windmill is still in service in the farmlands of northern France.

province, as they border many of the busiest waterways of the region. While Normandy's main features are flooded valleys and seaports, the city of Avranches, in the southwest corner of Manche, offers perfect views of the scenic and historic Mont-Saint-Michel, a rocky isle about 1.6 kilometres (1 mile) off the coast in the English Channel, though accessible during low tide or by causeway. The island is famous for its Benedictine abbey, founded in 708 by Aubert, the Bishop of Avranches. Mont-Saint-Michel lies just between the border of Normandy and the northeast corner of Brittany.

A Region Set Apart

Some people in Brittany do not speak French, or claim not to, instead utilising their ancient Breton language. This is in keeping with the history of the area, since Brittany has, even more than Normandy, always fought to maintain its independence and sovereignty. Around the year 500, a group of fugitive Britons settled the area and hence named it for their former country. But soon Brittany, like most of the rest of the region, had to overcome centuries of Frankish tribe invasion. There then followed other conflicts with England, France, and Normandy, until 1532, when Brittany formally became a part of France through marriage with the French monarchy. But to this day, the people of the region have maintained the ancient, pagan rituals of their ancestors, trying as hard as possible to avoid complete assimilation into French culture.

Like Normandy, Brittany also has its share of resort towns, beaches, and coastline attractions bordering the English Channel. To the west of Mont-Saint-Michel, in Ille-et-Vilaine, lies Saint Malo. It dates from the ninth century, when it was built out of a rocky promontory rising from the English Channel. Much of the town was destroyed during World War II, but has since been restored. It is a town more noted for its ancient relics than its modern facilities. Its famous old ramparts surround the island and offer views of the major landmarks of the area, including some large old dungeons, La Générale and Quiquengrogne.

Only a few minutes by ferry from Saint Malo is the modern town of Dinard, featuring immaculate

Following page: Honfleur was once an important port, serving as the point of embarkation for the first voyages of exploration to Canada. Today, its well-preserved buildings and cobbled streets make it a major tourist attraction.

Eastern France

*E*astern France delights the traveller with diverse pleasures: the sparkle of Champagne, the beauty of medieval cathedrals filled with intricately carved statuary, and musuems featuring objects such as antique tapestries and century-old automobiles—to name just a few of its magnificent offerings.

Champagne

To the east of Paris is the Champagne region, incorporating the departments of Aube, Marne, Ardennes, and Yonne. Beginning in the eleventh century, Champagne was under the control of the house of Blois, and in subsequent years, it became one of the most powerful fiefdoms in all of France. In 1314, the region was, through royal inheritance, permanently incorporated into the French domain.

The most impressive city in Champagne is Reims, about 112 kilometres (70 miles) to the northeast of Paris. The city's major feature is its magnificently elaborate cathedral, which, beginning in the twelfth century, took about one hundred years of steady work to be constructed. Nearly every French monarch from 1179 to 1824 was crowned in the Reims Cathedral. The structure was greatly damaged, however, during World War I, but with great philanthropic help from John D. Rockefeller, it was later restored. Reims is also of historical significance because it was the site where Germany unconditionally surrendered in 1945, marking the end of the war in Europe.

Naturally, the champagne industry of France is based in this region, with many of the major producers in Reims. There are wine cellars and tunnels all around the city, and they are quite accessible to tourists. To the south of Reims along the River Marne is another major centre of champagne production, Epernay. This town does not offer a very imposing appearance above ground, but it has an elaborate web of wine caves below its streets. The small village of Hautvillers, a few kilometres to the north of Epernay, is famous as the former home of the inventor of champagne, Dom Pérignon, the blind monk who discovered the usefulness of cork and the advantages of bubbles consistently maintained in the wine. The small village church of Hautvillers, which is all that is left of Dom Pérignon's abbey, contains his tomb. Another major town in the Champagne region is Chalons-sur-Marne, whose population is more than forty thousand. Even though most of the production is elsewhere, Chalons-sur-Marne is the official administrative centre for the champagne industry. It is more famous, though, for its thirteenth-century Cathédrale-Saint-Etienne, as well as its Church of Notre-Dame-des-Vaux.

The Alsatian town of Colmar is a popular destination for tourists, with its mingled medieval and Renaissance flavours. Seen here, one of the canals from the section of town known as Little Venice.

Eastern France, like so many other areas of this vinicultural land, is wine country. The great sparkling wine, champagne, was developed in this region.

The Strasbourg Cathedral, in the region of Alsace, dates back to the twelfth century. It is one of the largest Christian churches in the world. Its pink sandstone tower is about 150 metres (500 feet) tall.

Construction of Strasbourg Cathedral's astronomical clock spanned twenty-seven years, from 1547 to 1574. The mechanism in the clock has been replaced just once in all the years since then.

Alsace and Lorraine

Farther to the east of Champagne are the inevitably linked regions of Alsace and Lorraine. Alsace was part of the German kingdom for many centuries, but during the rule of Louis XIV, most of the land was taken by France, with the rest of it seized about a century later during the Revolutionary Wars. Lorraine was also fought over for centuries, passing through the control of the Holy Roman Empire, the rulers of Burgundy, the Dukes of Switzerland, and several ruling families of Austria. In 1735, King Louis XV acquired Lorraine from the Austrian Emperor Francis I. It became a part of France in 1766. But after the disastrous Franco-Prussian war of 1870, both Alsace and Lorraine were ceded to the victorious Germans, who united the two former provinces into one imperial territory. Following World War I, however, after absorbing an extremely high level of destruction from the combat, Alsace and Lorraine were returned to France, only to be temporarily lost again during the Nazi occupation during the Second World War before being liberated with the rest of the country.

The Alsace region, with its thriving capital of Strasbourg, its voluminous vineyards, and Vosges Mountains, has recovered from its twentieth-century traumas better than Lorraine, which lacks the tourist appeal of its neighbour and also is not as accessible for visitors from Germany or Switzerland. Much of Lorraine now stands as a continuing monument to the world wars that ravaged the region. The town of Verdun, where more than one million were killed during its World War I battle, contains many tributes to its fallen warriors. Its soldier cemetery, the Faubourg Pavé, was the location from which an unidentified soldier was picked at random and then buried under the Arc de Triomphe in Paris. Also in the area is the Trench of Bayonets, the Fort of Douaumont, and the Ossuary of Douaumont, locations containing hundreds of thousands of soldier graves. Verdun, though, contains more than just memorials to its war years. There is a lavish eighteenth-century Bishop's Palace still remaining, as well as the nearby cathedral, which dates from the twelfth century. Farther to the north near the Belgian border is another tragic city, Fermont. It was the base of the supposedly impenetrable Maginot Line, which, nonetheless, was almost instantly overrun by forces of Nazi Germany in 1940. The town is still full of relics of the period, including concrete bunkers, observation posts, and very intricately designed underground living quarters. There is even evidence in the area of the shelling the town took when it was overrun in 1940, as bomb craters still mark the grounds.

The two most attractive cities in Lorraine are two very old towns, the ancient capital of Nancy, and, farther to the north, Metz. Much of the attractiveness of Nancy can be traced to its earliest days under French control. In the eighteenth century, Louis XV gave control of the region to Stanislaus I of Poland, the father of his wife. This foreign monarch was originally not well received by the people of Lorraine, but Stanislaus did much for Lorraine and particularly Nancy, which, for its time, was considered a leading example of outstanding urban planning. Today Nancy still honours him with a main street—the Rue Stanislaus—as well as a statue in its most prominent location, the Place Stanislaus. With its famed iron gates, hotels, and museums, Place Stanislaus is considered the central square of the city. Among many displays of varied architectural style in Nancy, the foremost sights include the eighteenth-century twin-spired cathedral, mostly built in the nineteenth century, and the historic Palais du Gouvernement.

The city of Metz has a history extending back thousands of years, and unlike Nancy, it was a central part of the conflicts of 1870, 1914, and 1940. But its most famous structure remains, the Cathédrale Saint-Etienne, which at approximately 208 kilometres (130 feet) is one of the tallest cathedrals in France. Metz is also one of the cities in the country with the most grass and trees, including its most famous park, the Esplanade, which overlooks the Moselle River. The Alsace region is dominated by Strasbourg, which ranks behind only Paris in the list of French cosmopolitan cities. Its over 200,000 residents tend to speak a dialect which is a combination of French and German, which even those who speak those languages fluently find hard to understand. Its roots, though, are more German, and at least before the last German occupation, the road signs in Strasbourg were often written more prominently in German

The glory of Reims is its Cathedral of Notre-Dame. Note the scaffolding, visible in the lower left. The cathedral has had to be restored at times through the centuries. During World War I it was badly damaged by bombings.

The Virgin Mary beside the enthroned Christ and flanked by angels, sits above the main portal of the Cathedral of Notre-Dame in Reims.

than in French. This has changed since 1945, but more people in the city, as well as all of Alsace, still seem to speak German more often than French. Apparently, no one else in France is much bothered by this cultural difference.

Strasbourg has maintained much of its old heritage while also being the seat of the European Court of Human Rights and the Council of Europe, both housed in the modern Palais de l'Europe. The city's history includes moments of great significance both for France and the world. In the fifteenth century, Johann Gutenberg invented the printing press in Strasbourg, which still honours his accomplishments with its Place Gutenberg, home of the city's Chamber of Commerce. Late in the eighteenth century, in response to the threat of an Austrian invasion, Strasbourg's Rouget de Lisle composed the stirring *Marseillaise*, which soon became the anthem for all of France. Right next to the city hall, the Banque de France now stands on the exact spot where the *Marseillaise* was first sung. Like most major cities in France, Strasbourg's most impressive structure is its cathedral, the Cathédrale Notre-Dame.

Its fifteenth-century spire, built about two hundred years after the interior was completed, is over 150 metres (500 feet) high, the tallest in all of France. Other highlights of the cathedral are the statuettes on the pulpit; the organ loft, which rises to the ceiling; the intricately sculpted Angel's Column, which dates from the thirteenth century; and the Astronomical Clock, which displays Passion Plays daily. Right next to the cathedral is its museum, the Musée de l'Oeuvre Notre Dame. It houses old artifacts of the structure as well as the works of some Old Masters while maintaining the same holy mood and emotion of the cathedral. Strasbourg contains a great number of noteworthy parks and public places, including the Place Kléber, its central square. There are also the Place Broglie and the Place de la République. The idyllic park in the northeast corner of the city is the Orangerie, containing all the expected amenities of flowers, water, and birds, including such large creatures as flamingos and storks. In Strasbourg there are also other notable ecclesiastical structures, including the church of St-Paul and the church of St-Thomas.

Museums, too, draw visitors to this fascinating city. The Decorative Arts Museum features collections of furniture, porcelain, and tapestries, while the Local History Museum displays many relics of the city's past, including military uniforms, weapons, armour, and maps. Though Strasbourg dominates the province, there are other spots in Alsace worth noting, including the small village of Rosheim. It contains Heidehuss, which is more than eight hundred years old and said to be the oldest house in the region. To the south in Alsace is Selestat, which is famous for its two churches, Sainte-Foy and Saint-Georges. And yet farther to the south—in the southeast corner of Alsace—is the town of Mulhouse, which is the home of two famous museums. The Fine Arts Museum contains works of Dutch and Flemish masters, while the Musée National de l'Automobile houses more than one hundred years of vintage and modern cars and trains, including some rare, priceless models.

Colmar, 64 kilometres (40 miles) south of Strasbourg, is the third largest town in the region of Alsace. Its town square, pictured, is known as the Place de l'Ancienne Douane.

Many of the buildings
and streets in Alsace
are more German
in appearance than
French. A case in
point is the town of
Colmar's Pfister House,
built in 1537 for a mer-
chant named Ludwig
Scherer. It was
restored in the 1970s.

Following page:
Without question
the most spectacu-
lar scenery in all
of France is that
found in the Alps.
This mighty range
of mountains
curves its way
through most of
the southeastern
area of the country.

The Rhône Valley
and the French Alps

*T*hese bordering regions offer a mix of pleasures. For the connoisseur and the gourmet, the great wines of the Rhône and the fabled restaurants of Lyon await. For the sportsperson, there are awesome slopes of Alpine ski resorts. Whatever your interest, there is much to discover.

Wine Country

The Rhône is home to vineyards producing the internationally famous Beaujolais wines. In addition, the Rhône valley is rich in relics of its past as a Roman colony, as well as the castles, cathedrals, and unchanged villages of the Middle Ages and Renaissance eras. In villages such as Pérouges, the atmosphere of the Middle Ages is so complete that historical films have been shot there with very few changes made to alter the atmosphere. The legendary wine-producing region of Beaujolais is actually quite small, considering its fame and the amount of wine produced. Beginning a half hour's drive north of Lyon, the Beaujolais vineyards are approximately 64 kilometres (40 miles) in one direction and barely 16 kilometres (10 miles) in the other. In this area alone some 1.2 billion litres (30 million gallons) of wine are produced and sold around the world.

Visitors usually base themselves in the Villefranche and then set out to explore the numerous vineyards and châteaux, many of which allow guests to drop by and sample a glass of wine or buy a bottle or two. Depending on the château, the visitor may be taken to the underground wine cellar, where the vintage is drawn fresh from huge wine barrels.

A farmer walks with his horse and cart across a path near Vanoise. The hard-working residents of this area have little time for the sports and leisure activities that draw outsiders to the Alpine region.

The entrance to Auberge Rebelais, one of the numerous outstanding restaurants in Lyon. That city is considered the gastronomic capital of France.

Lyon

The largest city in the Rhône region, and one of the country's centres of fine food—the 'town that loves to eat'—is Lyon. Its recorded history goes back more than two thousand years, when the Romans founded the city in 43 BC. Lyon's location at the confluence of two main rivers, the Rhône and the Saône, made it easily accessible from all directions and a centre for commerce and transportation both by land and sea. The Romans utilised the geographical advantages and made Lyon their chief city. In the twentieth century, excavations in the area have uncovered numerous relics from those ancient times. Most of the discovered statues, vases, plaques, and the like are on view in Lyon's Gallo-Roman Museum, which is located near the ruins of the Roman Grand Theatre. This structure originally had a seating capacity of ten thousand and is the oldest Roman theatre in France.

Lyon became a centre of Christianity in the Middle Ages, with the archbishops of the city holding power into the fourteenth century. The epic religious gatherings of the Ecumenical Councils of Lyon were held in the thirteenth century. Lyon's most famous landmark, the Cathedral of Saint John, dates from this era. Today it rises above Lyon's well-preserved old quarter, which contrasts sharply with the city's otherwise modern appearance. In 1312 Lyon and its surrounding Lyonnais region were incorporated into the French kingdom by Philip IV. The prosperity that developed in the city over the succeeding centuries ended during the French Revolution, when Lyon was virtually destroyed during the reign of terror. But the invention of the loom helped restore industry to Lyon, which soon became one of the leading manufacturing centres in Europe.

An aerial view of Lyon, the third largest city in France. The body of water is the Saône River. In the lower right is the Saint Jean Cathedral.

Today, Lyon ranks as the third most populous city in France after Paris and Marseilles, but without the frenzied pace of those other cities. In addition to its historical sites and the exceptional scenery of its surrounding mountains and rivers, Lyon is also a cultural and gastronomic centre. It houses numerous art collections, including a decorative museum, a fabrics museum, and even a puppet museum. Its Fine Arts Museum, which includes many ancient Byzantine and Etruscan treasures as well as several significant works by Auguste Rodin, is ranked behind only the Louvre in all France for the scope of its collection.

Though the great restaurants of Paris may get more international visitors, the capital's gastronomes tend to concede that Lyon has the greatest restaurants in all of France. Food is a serious business in France, but nowhere more so than in Lyon. It is said that when a citizen of Lyon dines in another French city, the chef must be alerted in advance that a Lyonnais is in attendance so as to be at his or her particular best. The cuisine at restaurants like the legendary Paul Bocuse are such that visitors speak of them forever after. But it is not simply the marvellous dishes created in the restaurants that gives Lyon its reputation, for the hams, chickens, sausages, cheeses, breads, and fruits available in the local shops and market are all exceptional.

This statue in a Lyon park was created in honour of the centennial anniversary of the French Revolution.

A Tale of Two Regions

The regions of the French Alps, Savoy and Dauphiné, like many other outlying areas of France, were under the control of various kingdoms and countries before becoming permanent parts of France. In the Middle Ages, Dauphiné was a part of the Kingdom of Arles and ruled by a Dauphin. In 1349, Humbert II sold the region to Phillip VI of France, and for several generations, Dauphiné was considered a French province and was ruled by the eldest son of the French King. It was during the fifteenth century that Louis XI incorporated Dauphiné, including its historic capital of Grenoble, into the French kingdom.

The history of the Savoy region, bordering Italy and Switzerland, is more complicated. It was one of the regions conquered by Julius Caesar during his conquest of Gaul. Centuries later it was part of the kingdoms of Burgundy and Arles. From the eleventh century, it was ruled by the large House of Savoy, which also ruled a small part of Italy, all of Switzerland, and much of southern France. In the fifteenth century, the House of Savoy lost control of Switzerland, but in later centuries, it expanded its grasp in Italy, as the family went away from its French roots towards

Two rivers meet at Lyon, the Rhône and the more peaceful Saône. Here we see the Saint George footbridge, with the Saône's right bank in the background.

The rue St-Jean, once
the main thoroughfare
of Vieux Lyon, invites
the visitor by night to
enjoy the quarter's
shops and impressive
old houses, many dating
from the Renaissance.

Located a short distance
north of Lyon in
Collonges-au-Mont d'Or,
this restaurant continues
the city's great gastro-
nomic traditions. Owner
and chef, Paul Bocuse,
is known worldwide
as a champion and pro-
moter of French cuisine.

Vieux Lyon, on the right
bank of the Saône, is a
maze of streets, alleys,
and unique passageways,
called traboules, that
lead under houses from
one street to another.

those of Italy. The Savoy region was claimed by France in 1792, lost back to the Savoys—who by then were best known as the rulers of Sardinia—in 1815, and then restored to French rule in 1860. In 1815, returning from his exile on Elba, Napoleon wound his way from Fréjus in the south through the mountainous region towards Paris on what later became known as the Route Napoleon. Even today, the Route Napoleon, which winds through most of the major cities and towns in the Alps region, remains a well-travelled highway and a popular sight of inspection for tours and tourists. Forming much of the western borders of Switzerland and Italy, a great deal of the French Alps has been inaccessible until modern times. The advent of the local tourist industry produced new roads and cable cars, which made it easier to reach its many ski slopes, lakes, and spas, as well as the numerous natural splendours to be seen in its mountaintops and valleys.

Thus small mountain villages such as Avoriaz and Megéve—which are both near the Swiss border—are now popular destinations for winter vacationers, though they are also frequented in the summer for their lakes and golf courses. Megéve attracts worldly visitors during the winter, having become something of a hangout for actors, princes, and others who can afford its high prices. Avoriaz, still difficult to reach except by cable car, is the host of a Fantasy Film Festival every January. Also in the northeast corner of the Savoy region are the towns of Chamonix and Albertville. Chamonix is the largest French winter resort as well as the oldest (it was the site of the first-ever Winter Olympics in 1924). It also boasts the world's highest cable car ride, a 3,640-metre (12,000-foot) rise to the Aigulle du Midi. This location offers a great view of the tallest peak in all of Europe, Mont Blanc, which is more than 4,807 metres (15,781 feet) high. In 1992, Albertville, which is about 40 kilometres (25 miles) to the southwest of Chamonix, was the host for the most recent Olympic Games in France. Its venues and hotels were greatly expanded for the event, and so its facilities and lodging are the most modern in all of Savoy.

At their highest point, the snow-covered crests of Mont Blanc in the Alps of eastern France reach more than 4,807 metres (15,781 feet)— the tallest in all of Europe.

Grenoble

Grenoble is in the centre of the Alps region, along the Isère River. With over 150,000 people and numerous tall buildings, Grenoble is the lone cosmopolitan city in the region. It is a major French manufacturing centre as well, noted for its production of paper, cement, and electrical products. But Grenoble also has many gardens and sidewalk cafes, which give a lighter mood to the city. Additionally, with so many mountains and lakes nearby, the city offers a great deal of attractive scenery. Grenoble, the birthplace of the famous novelist Stendhal, also boasts a high level of culture and scholarship. Foremost is the city's university, which dates back to 1339 and has students enrolled from all parts of the world. Grenoble also has a Painting and Sculpture Museum, which includes works by Pablo Picasso, Paul Gauguin, and Henri Matisse. There is also a Musée Dauphinois, which displays a great deal of local arts and crafts within the walls of what was a convent, built more than three hundred years ago.

Inside Grenoble there are also many historic landmarks, including its cathedral, which dates from the twelfth and thirteenth centuries, and the Church of Saint André, completed in the fourteenth century. It contains the tomb of the famous, ferocious knight Seigneur Pierre Terrail de Bayard, who fought for France in Italy and was killed in battle in the sixteenth century.

Grande Chartreuse

Not far from Grenoble, and visible from nearby mountain peaks, is the Grande Chartreuse (Charter House) monastery, so huge that it covers 4.8 hectares (12 acres). The monastery dates back to 1084, when it was built by Saint Bruno. He was the founder of the Carthusian order of monks, who were noted for their devotion to an austere and contemplative life. The architecture of the Grande Chartreuse reflects these qualities. It remained the order's main seat until it was expelled early in the twentieth century, though the monks were allowed to return in 1941. For a number of generations, much of the Carthusians' income came from the green and yellow Chartreuse liqueur, developed long ago by the

The Alpine town of Chamonix, not far from the Italian and Swiss borders, lies under the shadow of Mont Blanc. In the area are awe-inspiring cable car rides that climb to within 900 metres (1,000 yards) of Mont Blanc's peak.

A storybook village in the province of Savoie-Mont Blanc. The Alpine province touches the borders of Italy and Switzerland.

The snow-covered slopes of the Alpine mountain range provide some of the best skiing in the world. In summer, the area is equally attractive with its spas, lakes, and high hiking trails.

monks and produced at the monastery for centuries. The liqueur is now produced in Voiron, a town a few kilometres to the west, where visitors can take free tours of cellars and distilleries.

Not every Alpine vista includes crags and snow. Here is a pleasantly green landscape, a meadow in Les Écrins National Park. Many come to this national park for hiking and communing with nature.

Spa Towns and Resorts

About 48 kilometres (30 miles) north of the Grande Chartreuse is Aix-les-Bains, famous for its spas and its outdoor activities. It has more than 10 hectares (25 acres) of beachfront along the Lac du Bourget. It is also the site of some Roman bath ruins, as well as a Roman Temple of Diana dating from the third century. It has now been turned into an archaeological museum.

Two of the most famous spa towns in France are Thonon-les-Bains and Evian-les-Bains, which are on Lake Geneva, or Lac Leman, as it is known in France. Both spas, with their huge parks and lakefronts, are along the Swiss border, with Lausanne and Montreux easily accessible across the lake and Geneva just a few kilometres away to the west. Farther to the south are a number of mountain resorts, including Bourg-Saint-Maurice, Les Arcs, and Tignes. There are many smaller towns in this area that can be reached by cable cars and chair lifts. Among these towns is the very fashionable winter resort Val d'Isère. About 48 kilometres (30 miles) to the west of Chamonix and Mont Blanc, along the Lac d'Annecy, is the picturesque historic city of Annecy. Beginning in the sixteenth century, this town was the seat of the bishops of Geneva—which lies about 32 kilometres (20 miles) to the north. It also contains medieval castles of counts of Geneva. Among other historic sights in this port town are its old cathedral and a château dating from the twelfth century. Annecy has maintained many of its old characteristics, including canals, arcades, and cobbled streets, which have earned it the nickname Venice of Savoy. To the south of Annecy is the town of Chambéry, the historic capital of Savoy and another town seemingly untouched by time. The most famous structure in Chambéry is its castle, the Château des Ducs de Savoie, famed for its stained glass and its replica of the Shroud of Turin. The most busy section of the town is its Place St-Leger, just a few blocks down from the castle.

The French Alps region not only contains the highest European cable car ride at Chamonix and the highest mountain peak on Mont Blanc, but also the highest mountain pass. Between Val d'Isère and the town of Bonnevalsur-Arc is the Col de l'Isèran, which is more than 2700 metres (9,000 feet) high. However, it is only accessible during warmer months, from July through October, though in those months there are still many stunning views of the Alps to be seen along this Isèran Way.

A beautiful flowering field in Isère contrasts with the distinctively shaped outline of Mont Aiguille, meaning 'needle'—some might question the name.

Provence

Because of its Mediterranean access, the Provence region may have been the first area in France to receive foreign visitors—or more correctly, invaders. Thus Provence has a longer recorded history than most anywhere else in the country. As far back as the sixth century BC, Greeks and Phoenicians settled the region with trading colonies at sites that later became the cities of Marseilles, Avignon, and Arles. Early in the second century BC, the Romans intervened. Julius Caesar referred to the area as his Provincia (province), hence its name.

Roman Ruins

Many Roman ruins remain in Provence, and are among the best preserved anywhere. These include the Pont du Gard, which is a very large aqueduct built by the Romans on rocks above the Gardon River. It was part of their system of canals constructed to supply water for nearby Nîmes. The ancient amphitheatre, or Arènes, in the middle of Nîmes, is not only still standing but is in active use, with a current seating capacity of more than twenty thousand. Through the centuries, the amphitheatre has been frequently transformed for other uses, but much of its original grandeur has now been restored. It is an all-weather theatre now as well, with an inflatable roof used to cover it during the winter. Nîmes also contains the remains of the Temple of Diana, dating from the second century, and the Maison Carrée, a perfectly preserved temple from the first or second century, which features a wealth of carvings and other highly praised Roman artwork.

Another town in Provence with extensive and well-preserved Roman remains is Orange. It, too has a stunning Roman amphitheatre—the Théâtre Antique—still in use. With its seats carved out of a hillside in such a way that provides for excellent acoustics, it seats seven thousand for various performances, mostly concerts and operas. Another Roman relic in Orange is the 21-metre- (70-foot-) high Arch of Triumph, which dates from the first century and honours the Roman warriors of the Gallic Wars. It stands today in the midst of a busy Orange traffic intersection.

The Romanesque cloister attached to the Cathédrale St-Sauveur in Aix-en-Provence reflects the city's medieval and ancient past. Enclosed colannades such as this were based on the ground plan of ancient Roman houses.

Following page: Vineyards in the hills above Saint-Tropez come to life in early spring. Many vintners allow tourists to visit and sample their product.

crime, crowding. But, with its mountainous surroundings and seaside vistas, it is still a scenic city. As the largest port in the Mediterranean, Marseilles is dense with large commercial docks for the freighters and tankers of the world. But its old harbor, the Vieux Port, is much more appealing and intimate, filled with pleasure craft and fishing boats. The most famous spot in Marseilles, high above the city, is the Notre-Dame de la Garde. This church, which dates from the nineteenth century, is generously endowed with sculpture and other artwork. It is most notable for its overview view of Marseilles, including the old and new ports.

Aix-en-Provence

A much more tranquil town, nearby in Provence, is Aix-en-Provence, known as the traditional capital of the region. The medieval city contains healing mineral waters that have attracted visitors for more than two millennia. The northern part of the town has roads dating from medieval times. They are charming, though difficult to navigate for some larger modern vehicles. The southern part of town is more modern. The main street is the Cours Mirabeau, often described as an intimate Champs-Elysées.

There are a number of cultural attractions in Aix-en-Provence, including a wonderful Tapestry Museum adjacent to the Cathédrale Saint-Sauveur. The cathedral contains a famous triptych by Froment. There is also a museum in town dedicated to the painter and native son Paul Cézanne. It features not his paintings but his studio and personal effects, many of which are recognisable from his work.

In much of sun-drenched Provence, the industrial world is forgotten and a more simple and relaxing way of life predominates. There is even time for a canoe ride through the picturesque Ardèche area.

In the hills above the Mediterranean sits the Riviera hill town of Saint-Paul-de-Vence, characterised by cobbled streets and tiny, centuries-old shops and residences. Once a favoured retreat for artists, it now caters to hordes of summertime tourists.

A tree-lined ancient roadway in Provence is the picture of serenity. Provençal geography and the quality of its light have long attracted painters to the area.

Les Baux-de-Provence sits high above a landscape of white limestone and green countryside. Half of the town is inhabited, but the other half, the Ville Mort, is a deserted collection of winding streets and ruined stone houses from the Middle Ages.

The Riviera

*T*he Riviera, also known as the Côte d'Azur, is France's splendid seaside playground, its various chic and sensuous towns and beaches known throughout the world as the ultimate resorts. The boundaries of the Riviera have become elastic through the years, but roughly extend from the Italian border, enclose the tiny Principality of Monaco, and reach as far west as Saint-Tropez. Along this stretch of the Mediterranean there are large cities and tiny ports; quiet, exclusive bastions of the very wealthy and frenetic stomping grounds of footloose youths. There are museums and landmarks and assorted cultural attractions in this part of France, but the undeniable lure is the sun and the sea.

Before World War II, the Riviera was primarily a winter resort to which people came to take advantage of the relatively balmy climate. The tourist trade at that time was made up almost entirely of the ultrawealthy, with a sprinkling of artists' colonies to keep things interesting. Since the war, the high season has shifted to the summer months, when the weather is dependably warm and dry, offering long days of sunshine and comfortable ocean bathing. And while the rich still maintain in their enclaves, the Azure Coast has democratised its image considerably, with areas catering to more budget-conscious families and students.

Menton and the Coastline

The city of Menton, at the borderline, is a rich mixture of the French and Italian cultures. In winter it is known as the warmest spot on the Riviera and continues to get a sizable number of off-season visitors, mostly retirees. The poet and filmmaker Jean Cocteau spent a great deal of time in Menton,

The city of Nice is renowned for its fine restaurants and the quality of its cuisine, a tantalising amalgam of French and Italian.

The Riviera port town of Villefranche is a quiet neighbour to busy Nice. Through the years the town has attracted many writers and artists, including Aldous Huxley and Jean Cocteau.

Revellers in the trendy Riviera resort of Saint-Tropez take
a few moments for quiet contemplation at sunset.
St-Trop's nightlife is as famous as its glorious Tahiti Beach.

and a small fort has been turned into a museum showcasing his manuscripts, personal effects, and portraits. The roads west, called the Corniches, were carved out of the rugged mountainsides rising just behind the coastline. These elevated and precarious roadways have been the site of many deadly accidents, perhaps in part because the view looking down at the coast is so spectacular that drivers may tend to become fatally distracted. The coastal road passes through the tiny nation of Monaco, a leftover from the days when feudal fiefdoms dotted the European landscape. Its capital, Monte Carlo, is a tourist attraction primarily for its huge casino of legend.

Farther along the coast you come to the charming village of Saint-Jean-Cap-Ferrat on the lush peninsula of Cap Ferrat, whose residential lanes contain villas occupied by movie stars, monarchs (exiled and otherwise,) and other celebrated figures. A longtime resident was the late British novelist Somerset Maugham, his home recognisable by his arched insignia still visible on the outer wall.

Nice

Nice is the Riviera resort for those who like to mix their swimming with all the attractions—and peril—of the big city. Next to Marseilles it is the largest city on the south coast of France. For all its hectic activity and traffic congestion, many find it a pleasurable destination for a holiday in the sun. The seaside is bordered by a sweeping walkway, the Promenade des Anglaise; there is plenty of nightlife; and prices are relatively reasonable compared to other Riviera hotspots.

For sun worshippers making their first trip to Nice, the biggest surprise—some would say disappointment—is that the city's long, arching public beach is made of rocks, not sand. Still, the charm of the city draws visitors year-round, and many visit the Tour Bellanda to be treated to an eagle's-nest view of the beach, promenade, and sea of colourful tiled rooftops. Another reason to pay a visit is that

The deluxe Hôtel Negresco is a landmark along Nice's beachfront boulevard, the Promenade des Anglaise. Although many people take their vacations in Nice, it is a large and busy city, rather than a subdued resort.

each year, a dozen days before Shrove Tuesday, Nice hosts a Carnival, one of the largest and liveliest of its kind in the world. There is even an attraction for art lovers in Nice: The state-run Chagall Museum, located in the hills above the city, is a unique showcase for the Russian-born painter's work.

Cannes, Saint-Tropez and Other Destinations

Travelling west from the big city, one finds numerous charming small port towns and ancient hillside villages. For many travellers these tranquil and beautiful locales are far superior destinations to the better-known and overdeveloped resorts along the Riviera. Facing Nice across the Bay of Angels is the old port of Antibes. The town contains a Picasso Museum featuring hundreds of pieces that the prolific painter created while a local resident. The peninsula jutting to the south—Cap d'Antibes—is the domain of the rich and famous, with its massive villas and legendary lodgings on the rocks, the Hôtel du Cap.

Juan-les-Pins, northwest of the cape, was once another exclusive domain of the rich, a chic resort for cafe society in prewar days. It still retains a certain cachet, though its wild nightlife is anything but staid or exclusive. Its annual jazz festival is renowned. The town's name, in English 'John's Pines', refers to the abundant pine trees in the area. Heading west, there are more picturesque ports and quiet hill towns to explore.

The next major destination on the map is Cannes, a big and busy city with a sumptuous beachfront boulevard, the Promenade de la Croisette. The landmark among the beachfront properties is the Carlton Hotel, an elegant white building that is to some like a giant wedding cake. Cannes's celebrated name among the Riviera's crown jewels is due largely to the annual presence of the film festival. Each spring, the festival turns Cannes into a frenzied convention hall for the motion picture business, crowding every street, hotel, restaurant, cafe, theatre, and practically each grain of the sandy beach with film stars, producers, directors, reporters, photographers, and gawkers and hustlers of every description. There is no better view of the cinema's mix of art, glamour, and

The Carlton, in the city of Cannes, is one of the legendary luxury hotels of the French Riviera. To some, the white-painted structure resembles a wedding cake. An impressive number of international film stars have stayed there.

The Riviera resort of Cannes is best known as the annual site of the International Film Festival. For two weeks in May, the city surrenders itself to hordes of filmmakers, photographers, reporters, movie fans, and aspiring starlets posing for anyone who will point a camera lens in their direction.

Following page:
Once a sleepy fishing port treasured by a côterie of visiting artists, Saint-Tropez's charms were shown to the world in And God Created Woman, *the film sensation of the 1950s starring Brigitte Bardot. The actress continues to have a residence outside of town.*

The Monte Carlo harbour in the Principality of Monaco draws an international crowd. At right, just above the sea, is the legendary Casino. In the last decade, highrise buildings have been added to tiny Monaco's skyline--some say to its detriment.

commerce than in those ten days or so at Cannes. The attending media circus operates at a single frenzied level, whether covering a major festival premiere or a starlet doing a striptease beside the sea.

Those seeking an escape from the high life of Cannes could do no better than a visit to the resort villages of Mandelieu-La Napoule. Here one can swim and dine in an evocative setting with a medieval château looming over the beach; it is now a museum featuring the work of sculptor Henry Clews.

The traditional Riviera has been extended ever farther west by the rising popularity of a once-obscure fishing village called Saint-Tropez. The coterie of painters and writers who had known of Saint-Tropez's charm and magnificent beaches saw their secret place revealed to the world when a low-budget French film—*And God Created Woman*, starring a young and frequently nude Brigitte Bardot and filmed on St-Trop's golden sands—became a huge international success. As young and trendy crowds continued to pour in throughout the 1960s, Saint-Tropez became permanently altered, with its rock 'n' roll nightlife and sensual Tahiti Beach making it a magnet for fashionable hedonists.

The resorts along the Mediterranean continue right to Marseilles and include such unique destinations as the Île du Levant, a tiny offshore island for nudists. Most spots on this beautiful coastline, even those towns not well known to international visitors, have been long ago discovered and developed for the hordes of French vacationers who abandon the rest of the country each August for a month in the sun.

Despite the presence of other vacationers, the beauty of this part of the world is so abundant that you should not have too much trouble finding your personal Riviera paradise.

Built on a high promontory overlooking Monte Carlo is the grand palace. It is the residence of the Grimaldi, Monaco's ruling family. The son and daughters of the reigning Prince Rainier and his late wife, Princess Grace (the former movie star Grace Kelly), are the subjects of much gossip in the international press.

Southwest France

The southwest region of France, combining French traditions with those of Spain and the distinctive Basques, is perhaps the most culturally diverse in the entire country.

Aquitaine (Guienne)

The old Aquitaine region—comprising an area later known as Guienne—and in particular its major city of Bordeaux, has historically been a major hub in France because of its location along the Garonne River, which flows into the region from the southwest, and the Gironde, which provides access from the Atlantic Ocean, about 96 kilometres (60 miles) to the north of Bordeaux.

Aquitane has a rich history dating back to the days of Roman rule, when Bordeaux—then known as Burdigala—was the provincial capital. Like most of the country, the region was later taken over by the Visigoths and then the Franks before becoming a French duchy in the ninth century. In the twelfth century, the region was lost to France through the marriage of Eleanor of Aquitane to the English King Henry II. The province was finally reclaimed by France more than three centuries later at the end of the Hundreds' Year War. During the period of both World Wars, Bordeaux served as an emergency capital for the country.

A medieval tower bridge in the town of Cahors illustrates its ancient heritage. What makes travel in provincial France so enjoyable is the active presence of so many ancient structures such as this.

The modern city of Bordeaux has a population in excess of a quarter million. The most striking feature of the city is its eighteenth century architecture. Most prominent is the elegant and monumental Grand Thêatre, designed by Victor Louis and completed in 1780. Its exterior is elaborately designed and its theatre hall contains a huge chandelier of Bohemian crystal, which hangs down from the heavily frescoed ceiling. Another prominent eighteenth-century structure within Bordeaux is its central square near the Caronne River, the Place de la Bourse. Other noteworthy sights within the city are the town hall, with its lush surrounding gardens, and the Fine Arts Museum, which has an extensive collection of works from the fifteenth century to the present.

As compelling as its history and architecture may be, Bordeaux is, of course, best known for its production of wine. In the surrounding region are such prominent

The colourful harbour of St-Jean-de-Luz has been vital to the town since its beginning. Today this old fishing port attracts visitors who come to enjoy the many historic buildings and fine beach.

Workers in Bordeaux region vineyards harvest grapes in autumn. Afterward, the grapes undergo a complex process that eventually results in wine.

Fruits of the vine harvested in a Bordeaux region vineyard will be transformed into wine of international repute.

This unusual church, located in the town of Saint-Emilion, was hewn out of the rock face by the Benedictine monks between the ninth and twelfth centuries.

vineyards as those of Médoc, Sauternes, Graves and Entre-Deux-Mers. Within Bordeaux is the CIVB, the headquarters and information centre of the wine industry, which also offers samples of the local products. The nearby Vinotèque sells Bordeaux wines in a huge variety of tastes and costs.

Epicurean Delights

In addition to its vineyards, this region and the southern Atlantic coast are well known for producing some of France's greatest delicacies, such as oysters, truffles, and foie gras, along with supreme fruits and vegetables. There are a number of beautiful sites in the region offering glimpses of the past and vistas of timeless beauty. Among noteworthy towns in the area are Saint Savin, with its beautiful eleventh-century abbey, and Poitiers in Vienne, famous for its Romanesque church, and Cognac, where the exquisite drink of the same name has been produced for more than four hundred years. To the north is the quaint town of La Rochelle. Its historic harbour is flanked by two large fortresses constructed in the fourteenth century. La Rochelle was the last stronghold of the Huguenots, falling to Richelieu's forces in 1628. During World War II, the occupying German forces used the town as a submarine base, but La Rochelle was spared any war damage.

Twilight at the village of La Rochelle, and the fishing boats return with their day's catch. Fresh seafood is, naturally enough, a speciality of the local restaurants.

A vendor in one of Bayonne's arcade shops prepares his display of cheeses. The variety of cheeses produced in France is so great that no shop could ever claim to offer all of them.

The ancient Romans were great builders, and countless of their constructions are still seen throughout southern France. A fine example is Pont du Gard, circa 18 BC, a three-tier aqueduct spanning the Gardon River in the Languedoc region.

The Basque region of France, on the border with Spain, reflects many customs of its neighbour, such as 'running of the bulls'.

The Basques of France maintain many of their old customs and have a thriving, distinct folklore. Here, Basque men—some in the traditional red berets—perform the 'Good Versus Evil' Pastorale in the Zuberoa region.

Basque Country and the Pyrénées

To the south and along the border with Spain is France's Basque country. The region includes much of the Pyrénées mountain range, the Basque culture ignoring the imposed national borders and extending far into Spain. There are over 200,000 French Basques, most speaking their own language and maintaining their own distinct customs. The majority live as farmers, fishermen, and shepherds. The main port in this area is Bayonne, on the Adour and Nive Rivers near the Bay of Biscay—it is considered the gateway to Basque country. Bayonne—where the bayonet was invented more than three hundred years ago—includes museums of fine arts and Basque folklore.

The great resort of France's southwestern Atlantic coast is Biarritz, a legendary seaside playground for the rich and royal in the nineteenth century, popularised by Napoleon III, who frequently took his holidays there. Biarritz continues to be a popular and elegant resort, though it has been rather over-shadowed by the trendier Riviera resorts in our era.

The Pyrénées mountain range is the second largest in Europe. Nestled within this area of mountains, rivers, and lakes is the famous winter resort of Pau, a favourite of nineteenth-century English

On the outskirts of the town of Ustaritz, the Nive River flows with the Pyrénées in the distance. Many sports-men come here for the excellent fishing.

vacationers. It is also the area of the sacred site of Lourdes. In 1858, a miller's daughter named Bernadette claimed to have seen the Virgin Mary inside a grotto near the local Gave du Pau river and soon saw water springing up there. Since then, millions of the sick and handicapped and other believers have made a pilgrimage to the holy site and its supposedly healing waters.

To the northeast of the Pyrénées region is the area known as Languedoc, an old province containing such distinctive cities as Carcassone, home to a stunning walled city dating from the fifth century. Nîmes, with its bull-fighting arena, lies just over the Provence border.

Toulouse is also a major city, a university town with a vibrant nightlife. It was the capital of the Visigoths during their rule in the fifth and sixth centuries. After many religious wars, the region passed to France in the thirteenth century. Besides the architectural remnants of the past, Toulouse offers a bit of human continuity in its poetry contest, an annual event dating back to the year 1323. The most famous landmark in Toulouse is the basilica of Saint-Sernin, which dates from the eleventh century. Other highlights of Toulouse are its Cathedral of Saint-Étienne, with its magnificent tapestries, and the central square of the city, Place du Capitole, with its beautiful city hall building. Place Wilson, with its atmospheric square and building, is one of the city's major meeting places, an elegant focal point, filled with atmospheric cafes.

Following page: A farmstead in the region of Lapurdi sits in the shadow of the Pyrénées. This is a region that is home to the distinctive culture of the Basques.

The Capitole Building in Toulouse was built in 1753. In addition to housing the city government the building contains a good-sized theatre.

Toulouse, in the southern province of Languedoc, is the fourth largest city in France. It is known for its red brick buildings.

A million pilgrims annually visit the city of Lourdes, where a young shepherd girl, Bernadette Soubirous, is believed to have seen a vision of the Virgin Mary. Many visitors come to be cured of ailments and handicaps.

A very up-to-date train prepares to leave the platform at the station in the city of Bayonne. France has one of the world's most efficient and extensive railway systems.

*At the southern end of France's Atlantic coastline, near the Spanish border, is
the lovely resort town of Biarritz. Visitors can stay at the luxurious Hôtel du Palais,
an actual palace built by Napoleon III for his wife, the Empress Eugénie.*

A closeup view of one of the gargoyles on the façade of Saint Mary's Cathedral in Bayonne reveals its similarity to the more famous monstrosities on Paris' Notre Dame.

Bayonne is the capital of the Basque region of southeastern France. Its most notable landmark is seen here—the thirteenth-century Gothic-designed Saint Mary's Cathedral.

*Languedoc is a watery area of France, its rivers fed by
the Rhône. Toulouse and Nîmes—considered by some to be part of
Provence— are the major cities in the region.*

**The lengthy Canal du Midi
is located in the Languedoc
region, an area famous
for its tiny white horses
and French cowboys.**

INDEX